MY TRUE FEELINGS

IN THE FORM OF POEMS..

ISHIKA SHARMA

"Poems" I love writing poems, when I wrote a poem for the first time I was not aware of that I am writing a poem I realised it after writing it. My first poem was dedicated to my bestfriends . I have 5 bestfriends from my childhood , but now we aren't living in a same area . Remembering all our memories I was a bit sad and I started writing a poem with deep and true feelings..

In this way my journey to become a poet begins .. I just wish all the readers are going to read my poems with so truely feelings.

Contents

Foreword *vii*

Preface *ix*

1. Best Friends 1

2. Stars 2

3. A Horrible Dream 3

4. Life Is Like An Ocean 4

Foreword

This book is totally filled up with my deep feelings and attachments . Maximum poems in this book are some true events I have gone through in my life .

I am Ishika , my home town is located in Odisha. I live in a town area so I can easily enjoy the beauty of nature , with calmness I write poems .

I am very thankful to all readers and I hope you will love all the poems.

Preface

There are four poems in this book and I just hope readers will feel the poem very beautifully....

1. BEST FRIENDS

You my childhood friend , we grew up together,
I spent my most memorable times with you..
Swearing to be friends forever and ever..,
We walk together in a strange gait..
We went from sharing our things,
To talking and dreaming about fairies wings .
my all feelings to you I would confide,
having nothing to hide.
I have met a lot of people,
And also made many friends .
But none of them can took your place,
I only found you on the crowd taking my stand.
I know we seldom have a talk now,
But the bond between us remains still..
you are far from my place now ,
But still you are always with me , I can feel....
- Ishika Sharma..

2. STARS

Alone in the night I look at you,
Before going to bed ..
Oh! the shinning beauty of you,
The sky so full of shimmering lights..
Ahh! look that very far away ,
Another looks like the very same one .
And silent wonders what to say?
Do you gaze into the sky at night..
To the stars that watch over me ,
Do you listen to my sighs ..
My calculated good byes,
My I will leave now threats ,
And I"ll be there promises..
- Ishika Sharma

3. A HORRIBLE DREAM

When I watched a dream in excite,
That dream in my memory is still bright.
I was in an empty room ,
And then a sound from outsides comes "boom"!
I went outside and saw, the vase was fallen from a height,
No worry , I felt it's alright.
Someone called up my name ,
in a rough voice, I ran to find any place .
I felt my breath tight ,
And exactly at the corner of my right..
There was a woman with forced smile; staring eyes
Looking deep behind my sight..
I was so fearing too see ,
and then she came near to me .
I closed my eyes, a soft hand touched me,
Mom was near me saying " Dear it was nothing just a dream ."
- Ishika Sharma

4. LIFE IS LIKE AN OCEAN

Sitting alone in the beach,
I realised many things .
Life is like an ocean,
But I have an edge to reach.
I am lost in the ocean of memories,
It comes in waves ebbing and flowing.
Learn from the waves ,
And enjoy the ride.
The waves whisper to me ,
Calling me to the soft sand .
The water sweeps over my feet,
Surrounds where I stand .
I neither see any begining ,
Nor I see any end .
I am floating over a body ,
even my body is not my friend .
I will leave this body a day ,
And move on to another site..
and then I realised,
to be more alive..

- Ishika Sharma

This poem "best friends " is the first poem written by me.

best friends we are miles apart but together in heart.. with so truest feelings I wrote this poem .

Long Distance friendship also exist..

Siting alone in the terrace ,watching and talking to the stars was feeling so awesome ..

Dear Stars, in the end when I will become a star like you, you will get jealous when I will burn and shine brighter than you...

This poem is based on a true event in my life..

Horror dreams .. it really feels like so adventurous . Dreams feels like it's really happening in real life . For me when I was a kid I too felt horror dreams as an adventure and excited one but now it's not the same. I just wish this type of horror dreams don't comes in my dreams..

Do you feel excited to watch this type of horror dreams or you too feel mm..not so okay or fearfull..?

Learn from the waves ..

Life is not about just enjoying , There are very different phases of life . Sometimes universe make a great change in your life but it doesn't mean your lifr has stopped . Your life going to continue making its waves like ocean. It depends on you that how you are standing strong and facing all the problems alone..

Printed by Libri Plureos GmbH in Hamburg, Germany